FROM THE HEART

FROM THE HEART

ry Lamb

To order additional copies of this book, contact:
Xlibris Corporation
1-888-795-4274
www.Xlibris.com
Orders@Xlibris.com
304908

Contents

Dark Nights.

Dark room, dark thoughts, dark shadows,
Sitting in the corner, mind spinning, distraught.
I see it edging closer; I feel it all around,
Don't make a single movement, or even make a sound.
They told me this wouldn't happen, the pills would make it end,
So why am I still fighting, the ghosts again descend.
Was I really such a monster, am I forever to be blamed,
Did I really kill them all, do I carry all the shame.
Am I the one who pulled the trigger, the one who took them out?
Now their faces come with darkness, in my head their spirits shout.
Can't go to sleep, can't close my eyes or they will find me there,
In my sleep I'm in their world, the land of dark nightmare.
Is this to be my future, filled with nought but pain?
Or will I win this battle and keep from going insane.

By Phil. M. Lamb© 5/7/2012

ANOTHER DAY FOR THE SOLDIER.

Slowly he opened his eyes, he could hear the heavy breathing for several seconds before realizing it was his own. The Darkness gradually turned to twilight as his eyes focused and he could make out his surroundings, the shelves with family photos and Dragon figurines. All grey now but soon the light would give them colour, he could make out his sofa and coffee table, shadowy shapes familiar to him. He let out a long sigh, "Still safe" he thought willing his ears to detect the slightest sound out of place before daring to move. Only after several long minutes did he move off the bed and cross the small studio flat he called home and into the little kitchen always alert for the littlest anomaly.

He felt them around him; they were always there even when they wouldn't let him see them he knew. He could feel their presence, in the air, the shadows, at times it was almost stifling. The dawn light started slowly to filter through the permanently closed curtains replacing the dim orange glow of the street lights, he daren't open those shades he knew what he would see outside. A draft whispered though the flat carrying the whispers of their voices, a subtle reminder he was not alone and would never be alone or allowed to find peace again.

For the thousandth time he asked himself, why did he survive and so many didn't. His family and friends say he was the lucky one, lucky, to have to live like this, to have to constantly remember sights, sounds and actions no man should have been asked to witness or commit. He needed a drink, his throat was dry and sore, as the kettle boiled he made coffee, strong, two sugars and a double shot of cheap brandy.

He used to joke that it was 'Fortified Marine Coffee', now it was the only way he could get started for yet another day, waiting dreading that he would see them again. When the flashbacks came you could see, hear even smell the hell again. The cordite wasn't too bad but there was one smell once you knew it you could never forget. There was no other smell like it, you could burn an animal carcass on a bonfire or a joint in the oven but none of that was like the sickly sweet smell of burning flesh, only people smelled like that when burnt. It was pervasive, haunting, this was how Hell must smell like, the Devil's Barbeque.

He went over it all in his head again and again, HOW had he got through and his mates didn't, and what was it for?

He heard the comments of the people as he passed them, he was the weirdo, crazy, and some would even cross the road to avoid him. As he walked he instinctively checked all alleys and doorways before going past, avoided crowds, hugged the walls of buildings and tried to keep to the shadows. He kept everyone at a distance, can't let them get too close; don't know who to trust or what. They could be and were anywhere, would come upon him out of nowhere. Sure he was the Lucky one, he took his coffee to his seat he could see the whole flat from there his back to the wall.

As he drank in silence the wetness again tracked down his cheeks, again he cried silently wishing it would end.

The feelings of an ex-soldier written shortly after a day and night of flashbacks, panic attacks and nightmares that periodically attack the sanity of PTSD sufferers.

PTSD is a mental condition brought about by witnessing or suffering a highly traumatic event in our lives, it not only effects the Service personnel in combat conditions but those involved in accidents, assaults and loss of loved ones. It can hit anyone of any age, and there is no known cure as such, only treatment and learning to handle and live with it. NOT everyone succeeds in this; some succumb, resulting in suicide. Most of us do not know it exists and fewer still can recognise it.

Many of the homeless you see today living on the streets could be suffering from this. It is an Invisible illness to most of us and I'm afraid to say, still not fully recognised by those in authority. It can destroy not only the person suffering but also their families, all are affected by it. It has been known to cause self-isolation, fear and paranoia. We hope by reading the works here many of you will gain an insight and more importantly, Awareness of this illness and in doing so, maybe even a little more compassion for our fellow men and women.

EVERYTHING here has been written by PTSD sufferers and their families. Thank you.

WORLD OF TWILIGHT

By Phil. M. Lamb

There's a world out there few will see,
A land of horror called PTSD.
A land that traps you within your own mind,
That makes the real world to you seem blind.
It comes upon you awake or asleep,
Forcefully plunging your soul to the deep.
No other human lives in this land,
For all are dead, hope drains like sand.
It allows you to leave now and then,
In order to haunt you again and again.
It never completely sets you free,
It lives to torture you, eternally.
Full of nightmares, flashbacks and times of pain,
It calls back the dead to drive you insane.
It lives and hides in your memory,
Deep within your mind, you can never flee.
Can it be exorcised, must I die to be free,
Or in Death be trapped for Eternity.
Another day for the soldier.

THE TRUE UNITED KINGDOM.
by Phil. M. Lamb©

The Bugle sounds across this land, and always we have answered,
We've never failed to aid our friends, never have we faltered.
We're proud to serve this little Isle, as it has always known,
She grants us safety in dark times, this Isle that we call home.

And though we wander far and wide we always will return,
In times of need we shall not hide, nor our Nation will we spurn.
If fight we must then fight we will, as Britons have through ages,
To aid our neighbours right to live, honoured in histories pages.

We're proud to stand, we're proud to march, and always hope for peace,
We're Sons of Man and while we stand, no Evil will we appease.
We know that when the task is done our government for us will falter,
We'll always have the warmth and love, of our mothers, sons, and daughters.

So heed these words you men on high, as you sip you brandy supper,
As you count your votes and profits rise, while you languish in false power,
You need us more, than you provide, as you hide in ivory tower,
The True power of this gentle land is little Tommy Tucker.

THE MISFIT

Now is the start, for here is night,
I sit here alone, in the video's light.
Alone I will think and alone I must dream,
For 35 years, always alone it seems.
I cannot mix, for I don't know how,
I used to laugh, I can't smile now.
I used to dance, and sociably drink,
Now I stay quiet, deep inside I sink.
At parties once, man, I'd be alive,
Now I sit in the corner and hide.
Drink I still can, most times to excess,
Walk around unshaven, always look a mess.
This change in me, I cannot fathom,
Can't understand, why this has happened,
Nor no I how to halt this sway,
That makes me alone, mind in disarray.
I try to tell them, to let it all out,
But who can listen, makes their stomach's shout.
No-One will risk to here the truth,
For in a soldiers mind, His memories the proof.
The horrors of war, in his head they all pound,
With conflict times, like Tumbledown.
No-one can help, for they can't understand,
So alone we are, alone we must stand.
But I still seek contentment in my life,
I seek inner peace and fun, not pain and strife.
I search for a life, both warm and good,
That has no hidden pain in it's cold dark hood.

By Phil. M. Lamb©   June 1984

Written for a friend who had just lost her twins in birth

A PRAYER FOR CAT.

My Angels up high now watch over me,
They're safe from harm; sing with me and the sea.
They stay in my heart; their sweet souls grow true,
Sing love songs and smile, we'll watch over you.
They'll always be there while I journey through life, Bring
comfort and joy, help me through strife.
The rising of surf brings your song to my ears,
The wind is your sigh that calms all my fears.
The Sun is the warmth I feel from you,
The bird's dawn chorus heals hearts through and through.
The Lord called you to him, you were so young,
He heard the sweet innocence in the heartsong you sung.
Too gentle and perfect for this harsh world,
He thought to spare you the pain life can hold.
Now I have my two Angels, they watch over me,
They sing of love as I surf in the sea.
They whisper comfort to me as I sleep,
Their joy and innocence in my heart I keep.
They'll always be with me, in my heart I hold,
They watch and they warm me, when times grow cold.

By
Phil. M. Lamb©   2008

THE LONG WALK
By Sheila English

Beautiful day, sun is out and sky so blue,
On this long walk, there's only me and you.
We take our time walking in the sand,
Walking slowly through No-mans land,
My faithful friend, I trust you so,
I will follow wherever you go,
You come to a stop; your tail is low,
Here boy!!! ... sit!! Lets take it easy.

My heart is racing; I'm feeling queasy,
I have done this job many times before,
It does not get easier, I know the score.
Job is done now boy,
Breathe easy; we're safe at last,
No British soldier will feel that blast.

TORTURED MIND.

By Sheila English

Anger, pain, hate,
Looking for a mate,
Tear falling,
Darkness calling,
Calm, peace,
Nightmares never cease,
Death, glory,
Same old story,
Comrades dying,
Their children crying,
Lost my friends,
Can't make amends,
Hurt gone too deep,
Can't get no sleep,
Tortured mind,
PLEASE BE KIND.

RELEASE ME.

DAMAGED GOODS . . . .
LONELY LIKE A WOLF.

By Sheila English

I'm baying at the moon,
Making wounded sounds,
The despair in my heart,
It knows no bounds,
The sights I've seen,
The places I've been,
You would not want to go,
You would not want to be,
Inside my head,
Looking around me,
Comrades dead,
Gunfire, smoke,
You almost choke,
Rotor blades whirring,
The wounded stirring,
I can no longer cope,
Don't seem any hope.

I WANDER ON, GOD KNOWS WHERE
HOWLING AT THE MOON.

WHITE HORSES,

by Sheila English 12/09/2011

Magnificent horses,
Running towards me,
Magnificent horses,
Come to set me free,
I grab your mane,
Made out of the sea,
I am a sufferer of PTSD.

We will ride through the sand,
I feel so free,
Running wild together,
Just you and me,
I am a sufferer of PTSD.

The wind is blowing,
Blowing trough my hair,
All of a sudden,
I don't have a care.
I am a sufferer of a PTSD.

My Magnificent white horses,
Will set me free.

WHY I WRITE

By Sheila English

I write when I'm happy,
I write when I'm sad,
I write when I'm angry,
And again when I'm glad,
I write when I'm up,
I write when I'm down,
Sometimes I write,
And play the clown.
Most of all I write,
Because I care,
And most of all,
I write to share.

A SOLDIER GETS HIS WINGS

By Sheila English

The sun is up high; it's a beautiful day,
A gentle breeze causes trees to sway,
I hear a sound, so sweet and low,
Where it comes from, I do not know,
I look around me; there is no one there,
I wander on slowly, then stop and stare,
At the single stone cross, standing there,
The name of a fallen soldier, whispered the sigh,
I'm watching a miracle, trying hard not to cry,
A new heaven bound angel is learning to fly,
The sound I heard was the angels call,
Saying, soldier don't worry, We won't let you fall.

AMEN.

REACH OUT I'M HUMAN TOO.

By Sheila English 14/10/2011

When you pass me in a doorway,
Why do you stop and stare,
Why don't you make the time,
To ask me why I'm there,
In a long distant past,
I was just like you,
Loving friends and family,
Plenty of work to do.

Now thanks to PTSD,
No one cares anymore,
Which is why,
I'm a bundle of rags,
You see upon the floor,
So next time your tempted,
Just to stop and stare,
Reach out and show me,
That you can care.

'THE OBSERVATION POST'

by Taff Evans.

With target picked I plan my op., and use a van to make our drop,
Silence is the key tonight, the moon the only source of light.
Drop off done, we wait a while, then cross the fields in single file.
Blacked out faces, heavy loads, we never ever use the roads.

The target house lays just ahead, no lights on; they're all in bed,
Dropping bergans, moving down, a final recce on the ground,
Finding just the perfect place, with line of sight to make our base,
All dug in and clear to go, I let the Ops. And Int. cell know.

Morning came and people stir, comings, goings now occur,
Cameras click and logs filled in, as men prepare a wheelie bin,
Noise of grinding from the barn, they fill the bin intending harm,
Booster tubes are set inside, the wires hanging down the sides.

Explosives packed within the bin, are driven off to be dug in,
The agents' words were very true, of what these evil men will do,
Success for me, my mission's been, the aim, to see and not be seen,
Info passed up through the chain, will stop these men inflicting pain.

Covert troops, they now begin; they track four men and wheelie bin,
The van has stopped, at this their goal, the bin pushed into waiting hole,
For these four men, their time has come, when now at last the ambush sprung,
You wait and hope and get the most, from this 'The Observation Post'.

JUPITER
By Taff Evans

It's early morning half past two, I'm woken up by phone,
You recognise the voice at once, that sad familiar tone,
"Jupiter", the first word said, confirm just who you are,
You've information of a bomb, that's placed within a car.

Teams are briefed, and then deployed, it's then I make my way,
To meet this man, this shady man, who's there to earn his pay.
Site secured and good to go, he sits there all alone,
The information that he has, cannot be passed by phone.

As I approach, I see his car, and park not far away,
A final check from all my teams, then finally make my way.
He tells me of a car that's parked, on farmland in a shed,
And where they plan to take it, leaving many people dead.

A man woman drive ahead, as lead car and as scout,
The driver with the bomb will wait, and move when there's no doubt.
The car behind, the bomb is there, to take this man away,
To save that sorry life of his, to fight another day.

The car behind must not be stopped for 'Jupiter's' inside,
I must ensure that no one knows, the secret that he hides.
For in this dirty murky world, of Ulster's troubled days,
Informers just like 'Jupiter', have helped in many ways.

The meeting over, now its time, to move right back to base,
And now I brief the powers that be, another special case.
Very soon the bomb, will move, the route placed out of bounds,
Then covert troops will sniff them out, just like a pack of hounds.

The men and women do this work, as agents of the crown,
You'll very rarely know them, yet meet them in the town.
Neighbours, friends or family, their secrets they will hide,
Paid informers, call them touts, you think they're on our side.

YOUR MISSION.
By Taff Evans.

Your mission planned, you cannot sleep, tomorrow is the day,
Your brief is to abduct a man, and quickly drive away.
By now you must be wondering, how safe your task will be,
Has someone talked, did someone hear, tomorrow you will see.

Your partner for your mission, you've never met before,
You only know him by his name, but very little more.
Your target was a former soldier, of the UDR,
It's him you have to bundle, into your ringer car.

It's time to go, you talk it through, time and time again,
The question always on your mind, today will I be slain?
Will undercover soldiers; be laying there in wait,
In just under an hour's time, you both will learn your fate.

You've finally reached the target house, the lights are on inside,
The target he is sitting there, a man who served with pride.
For both of you the pressures on, you can't afford to fail,
A thought that went through both your heads was, Have I left a trail.

Turning off your headlights, you drive up to his house,
Nothing moves, there's no one around, it's quiet as a mouse.
You draw your gun, you kick the door, your mission now is on,
Your aim is to abduct this man, then just as quick be gone.

You grab the man then threaten him, then drag him through the door,
A shot rings out, your head explodes, you fall onto the floor.
The driver is now panicking, he quickly drives away,
But bullets travel faster, and took his life away.

Your mission never stood a chance, for we knew all along,
The Det had planted microphones, one night while you were gone.
Your brief was heard, your car was tracked, we watched you from the sky,
You never knew what hit; we planned for you to die.

MY ANGEL.

By Taff Evans.

I feel a pain deep in my chest, Whilst on the battlefield,
Mum and Dad, I call for you, for now my fate is sealed.
I fall into the burning sand, my life goes flashing by,
Remembering all the times we had, for now I have to die.

Before I left to fight this war, we knew this day might come,
Today's the day we talked about, before my tour begun.
As I lay here, it seems unreal; I start to slip away,
The bullet deep within my chest, will take my life today.

I feel the medics work on me; they do the best they can,
But Mum and Dad, there is no hope, God has another plan.
He sent an Angel down for me, to take me up above,
My Angel wrapped me in her wings, and smothered me with love.

Mum and Dad, I feel so sad, it's time to leave this Earth,
I've done my job, I gave my all, my life was planned from birth.
My one regret, and only one, is to die so far away,
But Mum and Dad, I'll make a place, for when we meet some day.

MONSTER IN ME.
By S. O'Connor

I am lost,
Beside myself with fear,
I am not a lovely girl,
That many hold dear.
The reason why,
Resides in me,
It is a monster,
It is PTSD.
The reasons for its existence,
A tangled web,
One that left unattended,
Will leave me dead.
Of that I am scared of,
Believe it or not.
Another one lost,
To the statistic melting pot.
Faceless and nameless victims lost,
With their sanity, they paid their cost.
Are they bad people?
Ones sent to hell,
Nope, people like us, always mean well,
We follow the rules,
We try to provide,
The best for those we care,
But when left like this,
...there is no one there,
Go onto Facebook, pick up the phone,
But this is our head we are in, and on our own.

TIRED AGAIN.

By Christopher Paul Lavin

Tired again, not a good night with little sleep,
They came again for me, could not even weep.
Won't tell the wife, as she will start to worry,
Keep it in my mind, bogged down with slurry.

My body is aching, and joints are a crack,
Physical pain I can feel, take it all on my back.
Demons come while I try to sleep late at night,
Can't wait for the morning to come, and the light.

Feeling safe in the day, even when all by myself,
Going to bed at night, wife's picture on the shelf.
She keeps me safe, out of harms way, for sure,
An Angel in my arms, so sweet, small and pure.

That little lady of mine, know of my past life,
She stood beside me, not just as an Army wife.
My best friend, lover, Mum, and now provider,
I am so lucky to have her, she is my survivor.

Buzzing in my head, have I left the stereo on,
Mind games are played out, with a confusion.
Dare not tell or mention to my darling wife,
Face of stone, dark and cold, glad for my life.

RHYME WITH NO REASON.

By Chris. Lavin

My mind a filling drawer,
Full of facts and dreams.
All mixed, upon the floor,
Fell open papers and reams.

At a time, I was in order,
 Knew the job I had to do.
Memory, a great recorder,
And now a mess to undo.

Then came the dreadful blow,
Last time, would shed a tear,
Woke to find, no where to go,
An Angel watched over fear.

Just crossing a road and fell,
Now I cry, writing this bout,
Nothing there except a shell,
A quiet man without a shout.

Hospitals and Doctors, could not,
Tell me why this had gone on,
A seizure to take away the rot,
Family and friends > I have won.

Tears were allowed again x Thank you for reading.
I wrote this recently and is my way of telling about a seizure I suffered in 2003. A hard thing for me to deal with, as I lost my HGV license for 10 years. This has changed me, I lost 20 minutes of my life, I am still here and thankful for what I do have. Xcx C. Lavin

SIMPLY FUN.

By Claire Symcox

Its finally here, a night with the girls,
I bought a new outfit, my hair's full of curls.
The taxi arrives, we giggle and laugh,
Its always good fun, the laughs that we have.
We have a few drinks, discussions take place,
At the people who are out, the looks on our face.
Its quite disbelief, in the way that we stare,
At some of the outfits, these people will wear.

The nightclub is open; the girls are in line,
I'm last as usual; dear friend Sue takes her time.
We cross the road, My god what's that in my sight,
The car lights toward me, give me a fright.
I feel I am floating, that's just what he's done,
8 foot into the air, down to earth with a thud,
All these people, screaming my name,
Not sure why, am feeling no pain.

I hear a man say, "Just keep her face covered, it doesn't look good,"
She's starting to shake; she's lost a lot of blood.
Off in the Ambulance to the hospital we go,
Blue lights all the way, they don't dare go slow.
Doctor, nurses running all over, one has scissors, I scream and shout,
"Please don't cut my trousers, £30 they cost me, for our night out."

I drift in and out of sleep, from what I recall,
My mother and father, now there through it all.
I open my eyes; no more do I shake,
Hear a nurse shout, "Quick, Doctor, she's awake".
I look rather puzzled thinking it was only last night,
But 3 weeks in a coma, giving all such a fright.
Nurse asks me "Can you recall very much, when you try to think back,
18 minutes you died, and we brought you back,
But don't you worry young lady, you're on the right track."
I lay there quite calm, just looking in awe,
Here are my parents, walking through the door.

Three months have now passed; it's time to leave,
Bolts and pins in my leg, I now have received.
It's gonna take some rehabilitation,
I know I can do it, I have determination.
When I now think back to what I went through,
I thank you Lord, for not taking me with you.
For if you had taken me, on that day,
I wouldn't have, what I have today.
My partner Anthony and two wonderful children,
They are now my life, that's what I was given.

IN FAR AWAY LANDS.

By Claire Symcox

From a loved one at home to a loved one far away.

I see you in my dreams tonight the way I always do,
I see you in my dreams, because it's all that I can do.
As we lay there in each others arms, so happy and content,
It's a wonderful feeling, and it's how our time should be spent.

But you are off in far away lands, with no date of coming home,
And that is why I feel heartache and often, all alone.
You kissed me gently on my head, and said, "I'd die without you",
Ironic as it sounds, it could really happen to you.

It's not the way to think, I stay as positive as I can be,
Till I get that official date to say your coming home to me.
So for now my darling, take real care,
I will see you in my dreams, please, oh please be there.
I'll see you in my dreams, the way I always do,
And know this from my heart, I Really do love you.

A THOUGHT TOO MUCH TO ASK FOR?

Through city streets we see them, but ignored as we pass,
We try not to notice their dishevelled and huddled mass.
Many are rejects of childcare, or soldiers of the past,
But all we see are vagrants, the lowest of outcast.
We judge them by appearance, by the little that we see,
Spare no thought for how they got there, or who they might
have been.
The truth is hard for us to fathom, a truth we'll never know
A tale we could not bear to hear, that would make our stomach's
throw.
Yet we are here because they gave, of life, sanity and thought,
For our freedoms and our rights, these broken men had fought.
Returned full of nightmares, flashbacks, remembered once
a year,
A lifetimes horror in their eyes, yet we shed not a tear.
If you don't know what they have known, don't know of life
or death,
Then you should not judge them now as they fight for every
breath.
Offer instead a small kind word, respect they earned in pain,
A word of thanks is all they ask, they fought for all we gained.

By Phil. M. Lamb© 9/11/2012

THE CUSTODIANS.

Clouds roll by from distant lands,
Form magic sculptures, with mystic hands.
Drift over this green and fertile Earth,
Spread life-blood waters, help the seeds give birth.
They grow to feed the billions here,
Frail bird and bee, swift hare and deer.
These in turn, support the chain,
Of lifeforms filling the hills and plains.

Custodians of this world is man,
The surveyors of seas and far flung lands.
Who stride above all that they see,
The sun-gold corn and gentle trees.
Self-styled rulers of life and truth,
Brainbound species, so harsh and aloof.
Who enslave proud horse and passive ox,
Hunt the fleeting hawk and cunning fox.

Ambitions grow in their fertile brain,
To rule and control all on the plains.
To search, explore, and spread man's wing,
The conquest of life, of this Man dreams.
With wealth and economic states,
And force of arms and racial hates.
Change the lush green lands to barren wastes,
In the wake of their power seeking haste.

How will this end, will man atone.
Will this fertile Earth become sand and stone.
Will the clouds still drift over trees and grass,
And will the future of our green planet last.

By Phil. M. Lamb©

FAREWELL TO FRIENDS AND FAMILY.

Cast your eyes upon the ocean,
 Feel the wind over the sea.
Think of times when we have spoken,
Remember well of me.

For though I go to another place, deep in the mists of time,
My soul be bright and full of love, as I leave this life behind.
Undeserving I have been, of the friendship you have shown,
Of the patience, trust and love I've felt, from those that I have known.
In life there's been sorrow and pain, conflict and war abound,
All washed away within my heart, by the love of friends I've found.
My children shine within this world; in them I see the light,
Of a life of happiness and hope, of peace and all that's right.

Within my heart, within my soul, you all will remain,
For I shall guard, watch over you, until we meet again.
The treasures I have found in life are not wealth or gold you see,
But the warmth and depth of emotion, you've kindly shared with me.
It's the feelings found deep within, that builds and helps us grow,
The light of Man is within us all, I feel it, see it glow.
Though at times we try to hide it, covered in our fear,
We think that we might lose it, letting others get too near.

Each morning sun that rises, a new day for life is born,
A time for us to listen, and help new life to form.
To care and nurture friendship with those we know and touch,
To help those of us less fortunate, those down in life and luck.
I feel lucky to have known you, and proud to be your friend,
You've brought calm where there was chaos, brought pain to
an end.
But now the time has come my friends, farewell for me to say,
I leave behind my heart with you, to keep you safe while I'm
away.

Cast your eyes upon the ocean, feel the wind over the sea,
My life was brighter for your friendship,
Remember well of me.

by Phil. M. Lamb©

Written for a lady who I never told but has remained a close friend for over 30 yr.

FOR THE LOVE OF MY LADY.

With hair so dark and cream smooth skin,
Eyes, dark pools, hide the love with-in.
Life paints a picture, that shows in her face.
Each line tells a story, with each tear stained trace.

From childhood to teens, her way has been hard,
She can laugh easily, though not from the heart.
She longs for true feelings, but dare'nt set them free,
How I've loved this girl, though she'll never believe.

She searched hard in life, twice married it's true,
Had many a boyfriend, but none lasted through.
A beautiful girl, with feelings to match,
But the egg of true love, For her hasn't hatched.

From childhood to teens, her life has been hard,
She smiles very easily, but not in her heart,
She craves for some loving, but wont let them see,
I love this young woman, still she cannot see.

Time slowly fades the shine of her eyes,
Her soul grows dim, her spirit dies.
The years take their toll, with etched lines to her face,
Shrink her hopes and her dreams, in the march of decades.

From childhood to teens, her way had been hard,
She used to laugh easily, though not from the heart.
She longed for true feelings, but couldn't set them free,
How I love this lady, she would,nt see.

The saga of life, in us both marches on,
Lord Time, Lady Fate weald their power, then move on,
All life then must follow, the path they have laid,
That leads to the destiny, Fate has made.

From childhood to teens, her way had been hard,
She smiles so rarely, and hides in her heart.
Her lost dreams of happiness, her love almost gone,
I love you my lady, my hope lingers on.

By
Phil. M. Lamb© 2010

HOLDING ON
By Sheila English

On the edge about to cave in,
Must not let the darkness win,
People need help,
Cannot let them down,
Cannot fail them,
Must not fall down.
Must stat strong,
Letting them down
Would be so wrong,
Lord give me strength,
To keep up the fight,
Keep me from the darkness of the night.

PTSD, A CRY IN THE NIGHT.

By Sheila English

They are calling me a hero,
I really don't know why,
I doubt they would feel the same,
If they saw me cry.
I sit here in the corner,
Head held in my hands,
Thinking of nightmares I'd seen,
In a far off land,
Lord it's hard to be a hero,
When you're a wreck like me,
The night is so long and lonely,
I'm praying for it to end.
It's when I'm lost and terrified,
Please Lord, stay, be my friend.

SEPARATELY
WE ARE WEAK,
TOGETHER
WE ARE STRONG.
By Sheila English.

I lay beside you waiting,
For your nightmare to begin,
Your inner war tormenting you,
The war you cannot win.

I want to hold you in my arms,
Say everything will be all right,
Your not fighting this war alone,
Your safe in my arms tonight.

We lay together, side by side,
You're not alone anymore,
If we stand together,
We can beat your inner war.

WHY

As I wake each morn and greet the sky,
I see my battles and ask myself Why.
I've been back in my pleasant land.
For thirty years, never needed a hand.
Have always thought to earn my way,
Worked all hours for my pay
. Raised a family, but lived alone
, Can't let them in, need to alone.
Now told too old,
no work is here, So stay at home with all my fears.
Forever remember, forever to think,
Deeper within myself I sink.
Now I'm done, Have no more worth
Why the hell am I still on this Earth.
No use is then for this Dinosaur,
only because I fought a war,
but do it again for this land of mine
. To have peace for our young, and happier times.
I'm proud to have served this nation you see,
But, God,
Why can't they be proud of me.

By Phil M Lamb

TO DREAM THE IMPOSSIBLE DREAM

To sleep perchance to dream, some poet said,
He did not know about ,
The war going on in my head,
The images that come to mind,
The elusive sleep I cannot find,
A retirement present from the army,
Is it any wonder folks think I'm barmy
To sleep perchance to dream

DEDICATED To my dear friend Robert and all those suffering PTSD

S A English 2012

WHY

By Phil. M. Lamb©

As I wake each morn and greet the sky.
I see my battles and ask myself Why.
I've been back in my pleasant land.
For thirty years, never needed a hand.
Have always thought to earn my way,
Worked all hours for my pay.
Raised a family, but lived alone,
Can't let them in, need to atone.
Now told too old, no work is here,
So stay at home with all my fears.
Forever remember, forever to think,
Deeper within myself I sink.
Now I'm done, Have no more worth,
Why the hell am I still on this Earth.
No future is then for this Dinosaur,
And why because I fought a war.
But do it again for this land of mine,
To have peace for our young, and happier times.
I'm proud to have served this nation you see,
But, God, Why can't they be proud of me.

Respect is due.

Can you see the life I've lived?
Do you know the world I've known?
Will you learn from memory I give?
The seed of peace still not sown.

Am I a warrior of life that's bold?
Can you see the man, the shame?
You see a Soldier, or just a man old,
Will you feel, forgive his blame.

Men and Women are called to arms,
To fight, defend your freedom.
Their flown across this world of ours,
To battle in distant kingdoms.

We feel the shadows or our past,
See our friends die and suffer.
Live each second as if the last,
Our winter has no summer.

We stand to hold evil at bay,
A choice made above all other.
No second thoughts to turn away,
We stand by one another.

But when we're done and put to grass,
Back home, some left unwanted.
A little respect is all they ask,
They kept you safe, undaunted.

Phil. M. Lamb©

SHE WHO IS BLESSED.

She is the first face of love we see, the angel who gives us life,
She cares and tends through out our lives, sees us through all our strife.
Takes us on our first day at school, comforts when in pain or ill,
Blesses the tantrum and heartbreaks we feel, better than any pill.
Remembers always that babe in arms, even when we're grown full,
Patient to our rants when we think we know it all.
The Lady, the Angel, that binds us all together,
The giver of life and love, the best of life
Our Mother.

By Phil. M. Lamb©

PRIVATE GHOSTS.

by Phil. M. Lamb©

We make our ghosts, not just with gun, also with our memory,
With how we are, what we do and always what we see.
Men and Women of our race, have love, hate and society,
But still it seems when things go wrong we fall back into Barbarity.

I see them coming through the haze,
See them in the nights, Hear them in days,
I know each face and most their names,
They're in my nightmares, always the same.
As night time comes it brings the shakes,
Can't stand much more, my sanity breaks.
I lay awake, stare at the misty maze,
They all drift past, through my blank gaze.
The tremors warn of a relived past,
I can smell the cordite, I feel the blast.
Air is forced from my lungs and chest,
The lights of tracers race over the crest.

I made my ghosts, not just with gun but with my memory,
With who I am, what I did, and always I will see.
The Leaders of our race, use love, hate and society,
Then when things go wrong, Drag us back into Barbarity.

WARRIOR, OF THE RAINBOW.

By Phil Lamb.

He lives a mental life,
He feels a mental pain.
He cries in mental fear,
The world calls him insane.

He dreams of forests, green and tall,
Of doves and sparrows, bees and streams,
Of cool clean waters in lakes and falls,
Wild berries in bushes and strong oak trees.
He dreams of breezes, winds, soft rains,
Of night time woodland sights and sounds,
The owls in flight, ground squirrels plains,
 Not motor car fumes or concrete grounds.
He tried to stop the rape of land,
The destruction of woods and trees.
The building up of nuclear wastes,
That burn the lands and seas.

He died a mental death,
Killed by his mental pain,
For he tried to save this Earth,
But the world called him Insane.

RESURECTION.

by Phil. M. Lamb©

The time has come for this to end, to embrace the peaceful shroud,

I've now achieved my journeys end and leave this cold dark cloud.

My children grown, the world moves on, yet here I sit alone,

I cannot talk or tell my tale, my shame I must atone.

Emotion no longer fills this man, all now is dead,

I just look back through memories, of sights and tears been shed.

My life has never been fulfilled; Heartlove has not been felt,

The only time I fitted in was inside a weapons belt.

This emptiness must surely end, for peace to come at last,

To live this life as habit grown, with memories of a past.

To be surrounded by the ghosts of pains and hurts gone by,

To sever contacts, inside alone, I now join my friends,

Goodbye.

His eyes felt open, yet all seemed stark,

Shadows were swirling, cold and dark.

Was he asleep or had he awoke,

No one was talking, but something spoke.

The mist was clearing in fluorescent waves,

All spinning and floating, unfocused shades.

He thought he heard voices, but couldn't hear words,

Machines were beeping, is that what he heard.

A single word loud and piercing screamed, "STAY,"

Murmurs, then whispers, "We need you, don't go away".

The mists began clearing, Felt a soothing touch,

An Angels tears weeping, the grief, too much.

His heart started beating, lungs filled in a gasp,

Soon he was sleeping, her hand in his grasp.

I AM SICK AND NO ONE CARES..message for DWP

I am sick,
I am sick and tired of fighting,
I am sick of the daily struggle,
I am sick of the pain,
I am sick of the nightmares,
I am sick of people saying ,
You don't look sick to me,
I am sick of being told,
PULL YOURSELF TOGETHER MAN,
I am sick of doing battle,
OFF HAVING TO PROVE THAT I AM SICK,
In fact I am sick of being sick
BECAUSE NO ONE CARE'S,

I AM SICK OF BEING SICK ,
BECAUSE NO ONE BELIEVES ME.
YOURS AN EX SOLDIER........

By S.A.English ©

PTSD

I TOLD YOU SO.

By Louise Cater.

You warn them but they refuse to believe,
That one they'll have enough,
And eventually want to leave.

With all good intensions, they'll never understand,
What it takes to be there with you,
What it takes to hold your hand.

You don't need anger, bitterness or rejection,
You just want them to help you through,
Giving you what you crave, a little protection.

But most take it personal and WILL let you down,
Not realizing it's not about them,
When they see you drown.

They chose to blame you for something you never asked for,
The aftermath of C/PTSD,
It's rotted you to your core.

Very few will stand by you and realize this isn't you,
Too many will blame you for your outbursts,
And won't help you through.

You cannot control it, you cannot perceive,
How anybody could possibly want you,
And not eventually want to leave.

So you convince yourself, that this one too, will end,
You won't believe them when they say,
"I'd Never leave you my friend".

So no point in warning them, begging them to believe,
That one day they WILL get fed up,
One day they WILL leave.

When it's all over all you can say,
"I knew one day you'd go",
"I hate to say, I told you so ...."

ARE WE BARBARIANS?

We make our ghosts, not just with gun, also with our memory,
With how we are, what we do and always, what we see.
Men and Women of our race, have love, hate and society,
But still it seems, when things go wrong, we fall back to Barbarity.

I see them coming through the haze,
See them in the night, hear them in days.
I know each face and most their names,
They're in my nightmares, always the same.
As night time comes it brings the shakes,
Can't stand much more, my sanity breaks.
I lay awake, stare at the misty maze,
They all drift past, through my blank gaze.
The tremors warn of my relived past,
I can smell the cordite, I feel the blast.
Air is dragged from my lungs and chest,
The light of tracer race over the crest.

I made my ghosts, not just with gun but also with my memory,
With who I am, what I did and always I will see.
The leaders of ours, use love, hate and society,
Then when things go wrong, Drag us back into Barbarity.

ONE FALLEN HERO.

by Phil. M. Lamb©

Why didn't I hear the birds gentle choir,
Listen to night song, sat by the campfire.
Saw signs of Natures enduring truth,
The breeze through the trees, living proof.

How easy we miss the beauty of life,
To often we opt to see only strife,
Yet now I no longer need worry or fight,
I see natures magic, flowing and bright.

I see our medics rushing to aid,
Dodging bullet and shell to help and to save.
They work ever-harder not drawing breath,
Treat all they see, fighting off death.

Soon I'll be home, my family will cry,
As they lay me to ground say their goodbye,
We'll see him again; I know they will say,
Remember past times and happier days.

Now my battle is over, now I can rest,
Just lie here in peace see the world at it's best,
Watch sunshine pass through drifting cloud,
No man ever had such a pleasant shroud.

Do I have regrets, of this life, not at all,
I fought to keep freedom safe for all.
So they can mature, grow and evolve,
And find other ways, their problems to solve.

UNFINISHED STORY.

The room is full of sights and sounds,
I sit here quietly, and write of past times.
I fight the pain that's deep inside,
Within these words I try to hide.
I remember old times, both good and bad,
Remember past loves and hearts, I've had.
I sit and wonder, I think and dream,
To see my place in man's great scheme.

But my minds pictures, to me appear mixed,
Images and times, swirl around unfixed.
The flashes of joy, grow few and far,
Comprehension's door in my mind is ajar.
I see long ago a small boy of ten,
See his family group, but he's not with them.
He's been cast outside, and left on his own,
Chip grows on shoulder, heart turns to stone.

He grew into manhood, yet no-where did he fit,
The warm light of friendship, in him still unlit.
So he joined the army, a man to behold,
Find a place on the warriors nominal roll.
A soldiers life is both hard and fast,
Friendships made there are strong and last.
But their dreams are made in times of peace,
They shatter, as the dogs of war are released.

My career cut short, a civilian again,
I withdraw in myself, and hide in my pen.
Life turned unstable, my place twice denied,
You'll be okay soon the officer lied.
For the world out here is harsh and cold,

No room for ex-khaki is ever foretold.
You've served your dark purpose, now try to atone,
Live your life quiet, be apart and alone.

A quarter a century has passed me now,
I remember my past, through hard lined brow.
A son and two daughters bear the spark of me,
But always alone inside I'll be.
But what have I gained in my time, I ask,
Have learned of my future, from out of my past.
I cannot say, can't even guess,
I still seek contentment, my last quest.

By
Phil. M. Lamb© 1992

Written in praise and Respect for a company of proven heroes and veterans turned actors.

BRAVO 22 COMPANY

The world in general can't understand,
The price you paid, that war demands.
They think we fight for fighting sake,
That Warriors crave the Crimson lake.

They dare not face the injured warrior,
Refuse to see the pain and horror.
You tell your tale so they can see,
In such a way they cannot flee.

You honour us all with what you do,
And we in turn, We Honour You.
I sit in darkness, alone I cope,
I thank you all, you've brought me hope.

You told your story, you spoke to me,
You show your pain and we have seen,
Respect you've Earned, Respect you deserve,
Respect for all who stand and serve.

MY LADY SEA.

By Phil.M. Lamb, by Phil. M. Lamb©

Her moods are ever changing, deep blue calm to wild grey raging,
She is soft and cool, a mother to all,
But in anger, her wrath make the mightiest fall.
Her son thr Maelstrom, takes to deep the unwary,
Her daughter the powerful engulfing Tsunami.
Though cruel and harsh, at times she may seem,
She shelters and feeds, much life in the deep.
Life and beauty, in her coral and sands,
They swim, grow in wrecks among the ghosts of Man.
The treasure within her is not Gold, Jewels and silver,
But the rainbow coral and shoals of swimmers.
The Manta ray, and Giant Great White,
The Hammerhead, Turtle, Clown fish, coloured bright.
The Dolphin and Porpoise slender and sleek,
Lobster, Shrimp, Oyster and Clam, Sea-horse so meek.
She's the Mariners wife, the sailors wore,
Calls men to their dreams, from shore to shore.
The creator of lands and Glacial Iceberg,
Breeding oasis for seal and sea bird.
Without this great lady no life would there be,
The Monarch of Earth, Our Great Lady Sea.

LIFE.

By Andy Bannerman

As we sit back and contemplate,
On what we use to compensate,
Our lives as we progress our fate,
I wonder if in time we stake,
All on games we complicate.
The game of life has no return,
And once it's done our path is run,
But what we do as we go on,
Can further paths of those unseen,
And give to them a hope of life,
And futures known to gravitate,
Above the ceilings we do make.

PLANS.

By Andy Bannerman

What ever life decides to send,
Inside our heads we have a plan,
To conquer all without remiss,
And spend our lives as we see fit,
Whether right or whether wrong,
The plans we make can oft go wrong,
And in response, we remonstrate,
On all those things that change our fate.
And once again, we start again,
To prise away our common state,
And change our lives to compensate.

THINKING AND DOING.

By A. Bannerman

As we purue our dreams and goals,
We forget those things we know,
That keep us grounded to our quest,
To make our lives in contrast blast,
Of whom we are not, or whom we were.
And never do we contemplate,
Those things within, that from the start,
Stayed our path and gave us hope,
To build a future for the ones,
Who gave us life too, for our part,
But ne'er forget your stating point,
For doing that we will omit,
To raise ourselves as we see fit.

STATE.

By A. Bannerman

We oft sit back and contemplate,
Of all those things that do elate,
To run our lives and stay our fate,
And if we over compensate,
Those things we use to seal our fate,
Will never let us spread our wings,
And overcome those things we hate,
And never will we change our fate,
Unless we strive and duplicate,
The fact that we can change our fate.

PLODDING.

By Andy Bannerman

As we sit and live oue lives,
I wonder if we contemplate,
Those things that turned our lives around,
And gave us joy and hope untold,
To carry through those things we do,
That some may never understand,
Or even just attempt to do,
They simply live in apathy,
And plod along each living day,
So if you change those things you see,
Those ones that plod may come to be,
As full of hope as you and me.

MY ANGEL UP HIGH.

By Lorna Charnick.

Your face I've never seen, your voice I've never heard,
Your touch I've never felt, your hands I've never held,
You are the baby I loved and lost, so many years ago,
I think of you often, I've never forgotten you,
The baby I loved and lost so many years ago,
I felt my world had ended, the day that I lost you.

My armes they ached to hold you, but it wasn't meant to be,
They ache to hold you still, but I know it will never be.
There is a corner in my heart, that will always belong to you,
We will meet again one day, of that I have no doubt,
I'll see your face, I'll see your smile, And I will hear your voice,
Then I'll take you in my arms, and never let you go.

For the baby I miscarried, 26 years ago.xxx

VOICES.

By Gordon Spurr

The voices in the living room,
The voices in my head,
The voices when I'm in my car,
The voices in my bed,
The voices they are always there,
They never go away,
The voices tend to get me down,
I think they're here to stay,
The voice never make much sense,
They ramble on and on,
The voices aways wake me up,
I wish they would be gone.
The voices go on all the time,
They say such horrid things,
I wish always they would be gone,
Those voices in the wings.

THE OTHER WOMAN.

By G. Spurr

Oh I wish that we could be,
Alone, just you and me,
Not just for a few short hours,
I wish eternity could be ours,
While we are still young at heart,
Oh, if we could never part,
Think of the time that we could spend,
Doing things that need never end,
We could go for walks at night,
And return when it was light,
We could sit, just holding hands,
Listening to our favourite bands,
We'd go dancing in the rain,
Always happy, never pain,
We could fly out to the Suin,
And return and have more fun,
Time for us could just stand still,
Ihope someday, soon, it will.

D.N.M.

By G. Spurr

Doctors, nurses, medication,
Enough tablets to cure a nation.
One, tow, three, four,
I don't know what this one's for,
Five, six, seven, eight,
Take them now it's getting late,
Take the pills they'll make you feel better,
Said the doctor in a letter.
Don't take more, and don't take less,
Coz it'll make your head a freaking mess.
Can't remember what this one's for,
Bang my head against the door.
This doesn't work but I feel better,
Where the freak is that letter.
I'm in a mess, I cannot cope,
Even with this prescribed dope,
I need help but his costs money,
People laugh, coz I look funny.
Back to the doctors I go,
More tablets to stem the flow,
Of crap that's growing in my head,
I wish to f-ck that I was dead,
Doctors, Nurses, Medication!!!

CIRCLES.

By Gordon Spurr

The things that go on in my mind, are very strange as you will find,
If you could see inside my head, you'd see all things are coloured red.
The sky, the sea, they are not blue, they've taken on an orange hue,
The trees are black and so is the grass, no reflection in that looking glass.
There are bicycles with just one wheel, you can touch but I can't feel,
There's a broken cup with two handles, a petrol can, containing candles.
An express train that goes so slow, "What's over there?" I do not know.
Some where there is a greeting card, The stones are soft, the tissues hard,
Inside my head, as you have found, the voices are the only sound ....

LAUGHTER.

By G. Spurr

People laugh, they make me cry,
They think I'm mad, but don't know why,
If they could live one day of mine,
At the end, would they be 'Fine'!!
The price I paid was the Queens shilling,
I signed up, and I was willing,
Training taught us how to kill,
As young men it was such a thrill.
But what they can't, so do not teach,
Is how to cope, when you reach,
A pile of detritus that used to be,
A human being, that once was me.
I can cope but I don't know why,
I should even have to try,
To live a life that's full of horror,
When I was just a man of honour.
Doing the job, that I believed in,
Knowing that we had to win.
To keep this country safe and sound,
In the air and on the ground.
But when I could take no more,
I was kicked out of the door.
Left alone to try and cope,
No one there to give me hope.
I live a life of solitude,
People laugh, I think they're rude.

THE THINGS I LIKE.

By G. Spurr

The things in life I really like are few and far between,
I like to see the countryside in different shades of green.
I like it when it pours with rain and I get soaking wet,
I like it when the favourite wins and I have placed a bet.
I like when I have a thought, original and new,
I like when you're in bed with meand I say "I love you".
I like it when I'm fast asleep, all tucked up in bed,
In truth I think that I am dead.

SAND AND SEA.

By G. Spurr

To sleep and dream of sand and sea,
Wow that would be heaven to me.
I dream, if that's the correct word,
Of things that you have never heard.
Or even thought, ever could be,
I dream these things, because I'm me.

SLEEP.

By G. Spurr

I go to sleep at 10 o'clock, I wake again at 6,
When I awake I feel refreshed, my head is not a mix.
If I stay up late, there are no problems there,
I still wake up feeling refreshed and thankful for the air.
It is good to have a pattern of sleep and waking time,
Because of this I am able to organise my life along a line.

Then I wake and realise that the above was just a dream,
I went to sleep at half past 3 and slept for ages it did seem,
But when I looked at the clock shining bright,
It was still the middle of the night.
What would I give for a good nights sleep,
And not wake up feeling cheap.
And lonely, forgotten by the rest,
I trained hard, was amongst the best.
But now I'm sat here talking to myself,
Like the last bottle of booze upon a shelf.
Will sleep come, in truth, it might,
But for how long into the night.
Before I wake still feeling crap,
Would it be ok if I took a nap,
The nightmares come, one day they'll stop,
But will I, be here feeling on the top?????

GEORGE.

By Gordon Spurr

The voice inside my head asked "What did you do today?",
I wondered who was speaking, but didn't like to say.
The voice inside my head, became really quite irate,
It started shouting loudly, and hammered on my pate.
Then suddenly I answered, and everyone looked round,
Inside my head was quiet, I couldn't hear a sound.
The people round just looked and stared, some started to poke fun,
I would probably have shot, if I had had a gun.
I ran away and hid, from those people in the street,
I was so afraid, from my head down to my feet.
The fear was of hearing, the voices in my head,
I tried then to remember, just what the voice had said.
Then suddenly it asked me, if I knew that it was real,
I said "How should I know?", it said "Can't you feel?".
Then all at once I realised, that the voice was someone new,
A person that I hadn't met, a someone that just grew.
I started talking rapidly, to the voice inside my head,
I talked about the things I did, the books that I had read.
And thena strange thing happened, I really can't explain,
The voice became a person, and not just in my brain.
I called this person George, for reasons, I don't know,
And see him very often, when I'm feeling low.
We go for walks, together, my friend George and me,
He likes the things that I do, he likes the things I see.
We sometimes get strange looks, from people passing by,
Some people call us horrible names, it makes me want to cry.
I sometimes take George to the pub, he doesn't often drink,
In fact I only go out on my own, when I want to think.
If only people understood, what George means to me,
But can I introduce to them, someone they cannot see.
To me George is my best friend, he's always by my side,

I wish that I could show him off, and speak his name with pride.
People only laugh and sneer, when I talk to my best friend,
Some think that I am crazy, some think I'm round the bend.
I live with all these hassles, this ignorance and such,
'Cause in my heart I realise, that George loves me so much.
I'm sorry I must go now, I'm taking up your time,
But if you ever hear George, you'll know for sure, I'm fine.

I AM.

By Sheila English

You cannot see me,
But I am there,
I am the gentle breeze,
That's blowing through your hair,
I am the showers that in April fall,
I am the dove that you hear call,
I am the stars that shine at night,
I am the Sun that's shining bright,
I am the snow so pure and white,
I am your moments of sorrow and delight.
Everywhere you look,
I am there,
Although I'm in Heaven,
I still care,
Because I am all of the above,
And the rain that falls,
That's my shower of love.

I AM A NURSE.

By S.A. English

As a little girl, I never dreamt I would be,
A Nurse in the ranks of the British Army,
Never did I think that I would see,
The horrors of war played out before me,
No one thinks a nurse will cry,
When they see a HERO die,
I try to sleep in what passes for a bed,
Gut wrenching sights going round in my head,
Sometimes the Lord hears what we say,
And a hero lives for another day.
We are human can't you see,
We can still suffer from PTSD.

MEN, WOMEN, WE ARE ALL CASUALTIES OF WAR.

LIFE.

By Andy Bannerman

As we sit back and contemplate,
On what we use to compensate,
Our lives as we progress our fate,
I wonder if in time we stake,
All on games we complicate.
The game of life has no return,
And once it's done our path is run,
But what we do as we go on,
Can further paths of those unseen,
And give to them a hope of life,
And futures known to gravitate,
Above the ceilings we do make.

PLANS.

By A. Bannerman

Whatever life decides to send,
Inside our heads we have a plan,
To conquer all without remiss,
And spend our lives as we see fit.
Whether right or whether wrong,
The plans we make can oft go wrong.
And in response we remonstrate,
On all those things that change our fate,
And once again we start again,
To prise away our common state,
And change our lives to compensate.

THINKING AND DOING.

By A. Bannerman

As we pursue our dreams and goals,
We forget those things we know,
That keep us grounded to our quest,
To make our lives in contrast blast,
Of whom we are not and whom we were.
And never do we contemplate,
Those things within, that from the start,
Stayed our path and gave us hope,
To build a future for the ones,
Who gave us life too, for our part,
But ne'er forget your starting point,
For doing that we will omit,
To raise ourselves as we see fit.

OLD SOLDIERS.

Old soldiers never die,
They just fade away.
That's what the people think,
What many often say.

But they are all around us,
We see them every day.
In all our walks of life and work,
Who they are, we couldn't say.

We owe to them our freedom,
Our right to live our way.
They risked their lives to protect us,
With indifference to them, we repay.

Their lives have been distorted,
Their families become, estranged.
They could not take the nightmares,
In sleep they seem deranged.

The folks back home can't understand,
The stress they all endure.
To have to fight in foreign lands,
The reason why, unsure.

To kill is never easy,
The fighting often hard.
The opposite of all we're taught,
Childhood lessons from the past.

You change in character and thought,
Your world forever gone.
Try to live with memories of those you fought,
Long for peace and to atone.

They've nothing to feel guilty for,
For the task their duty took.
They gave of life for us you see,
We give them indifferent looks.

by Phil. M. Lamb©

A CIVIL ACTION.

We stand here together, yet each man alone,
We watched them coming, wish I was at home.
They marched on toward us, a horde of them,
Mothers with children, and cold angry men.
Balaclavas are worn, so faces are covered,
Molotovs in hand, eyes narrowed and glowered.
Hatred is felt, our fear we can smell,
Soon acid bombs fly, make flesh turn to gel.

We scream in our minds, but no sound will you hear,
We'll stand tall like statues, and dare not show fear.
For if we should falter, they'll pounce like mad dogs,
No, better their halted, by stern faced rocks.
Cold sweat runs in streams, down my visored face,
My senses grow sharp, heart n' lungs increase pace.
We're scared as we stand, tall granite stone,
Our muscles coiled springs, tense bodies groan.

The justice of this we do not know,
But we stand between them, the Prots and Provo.
As they face down each other, with bullet and blast,
But it's people that suffer, The innocent die fast.
Yet what is it for, this power play game,
The destruction of lives, for political gain.
At the end of it all, who counts the cost,
Counts the lives, and the reason,
the children have lost.

by Phil. M. Lamb©

Had a bit of a rough day yesterday, went on through the night.

DARK NIGHTS.

Dark room, dark thoughts, dark shadows,
Sitting in the corner, mind spinning, distraught.
I see it edging closer; I feel it all around,
Don't make a single movement, or even make a sound.
They told me this wouldn't happen, the pills would make it end,
So why am I still fighting, the ghosts again descend.
Was I really such a monster, am I forever to be blamed,
Did I really kill them all, do I carry all the shame.
Am I the one who pulled the trigger, the one who took them out?
Now their faces come with darkness, in my head their spirits shout.
Can't go to sleep, can't close my eyes or they will find me there,
In my sleep I'm in their world, the land of dark nightmare.
Is this to be my future, filled with nought but pain?
Or will I win this battle and keep from going insane.

By Phil. M. Lamb© 5/7/2012

THE UNKNOWN HERO.

She saw a man today, a man whose life looked shattered,
She knew she saw him everyday, but felt he hadn't mattered.
She'd passed him on her way to work, though hadn't really noticed,
He always sat in that same spot, a doorway covered with posters.
This time she but stopped and looked, his face drawn and thin,
She saw his clothes and crumpled coat, nervously knelt and spoke to him.
Are you okay sir, you don't look well, and almost ran away,
I thank you miss but I be fine, she listened, heard him say.
You see a soldier I once was, in times of fear and pain,
I'm home now and must sit and wait, and carry all my blame.
I answered my nations call, to defend all people here,
To keep them safe, so that they know not fear.
My time at last is at an end; I go to my reward,
Now tired and no longer fight can no longer bear the sword.
His head then tilted with ashen face the light in him expired,
A tear in eye as she held the hand of a Hero as he died.

by Phil. M. Lamb©

Look carefully I am there

GHOST OF A MAN

Wandering the streets,
Mister can you see,
I'm looking for the man,
That used to be me,
Upright strong,
That was me before,
Now i'm the drunk,
Huddled on the floor,
War ,war,
Bloody war,
No wonder
You can't see me anymore.

By S.A.English ©

TAFFY

Taff has written, I read each line well ,
Then I try to imagine the soldiers hell,,
Now I know why they sit back to wall,
It's incase the enemies bullet ,
Should come to call,
Why he jumps at every sound,
Waiting for the enemy whose gone to ground,
Every car a potential threat,
Smiling faces and yet,
There is murder in the heart
of those he just passed by,
Cant wait to see another Tommy die.
Every poem I learn a little more,
The terror of a slammimg door ,
Taff has written I read each line well ,
I am starting to understand TAFFY'S HELL

By S.A.English ©

PEACEFUL SLEEP.

By Gordon Spurr.

When will I sleep right through the night?
And not wake up, full of fright.
The sights, the sounds, the smells are real,
But you can't see, you cannot feel,
The images inside my head,
When will they go? When I am dead?

DARK SOUL.
By Sarah O'Connor.

Where once there was beauty, deep within a soul,
Is nothing left but a deep black hole?
The spirit was crushed by evils of life,
By wanting to be loved, without any strife,
Now the fire within has gone, all that is left is the dark,
No chance of light,
Barely a beating heart, which once so strong,
Now stamped on, and to follow it would be wrong.
So now I resort to using my head,
My ability to trust, is forever dead.

RICHES.

By Sarah O'Connor

I am rich beyond my wildest dreams,
Not with money or things,
But with love and friendship,
Immeasurable gifts, you cannot see,
But ones that allow me to be me.
I am blessed as I walk life's highway,
That I am carried, come what may,
Be it, I am floating up high in the stars,
Or in depths of darkness feeling my scars,
Battling demons, friends help me win those wars.
Always they're to truly support my cause,
Which is to one day, allow me to see,
Myself through their eyes, allow me to "be",
When that moment comes I know I have truly won,
And all the damage from my past will be undone.

BATTLEWORN.

By Sarah O'Connor

The sun slowly dances over the horizon,
Its beauty is something I keep my eyes on,
Remembering the days,
Fight through the haze,
Borne not of the Sun,
But what I did wrong,
The fog, omnipresent in my mind forever,
Its forecast, I yield to, just like the weather.
My thoughts, my images, my fighting for life,
Remind me of my past, not as a soldier, but a wife.
There were moments I smile on, as they are full of light,
My purpose for survival, they are what I did right.
My beautiful babies, made perfectly,
Though with little quirks, yet they stand by me,
Night after night, try as I might,
To hide my crying, as demons I fight.
Yet it's not to be, At the top of the stairs, they look down, see me,
So I shatter their peace and leave a legacy.
Of issues and fears, with me they surround,
Discarded, given into, the tissues scattered around.
My walls I build and try to protect,
I don't quite manage, though I need to, because of neglect.
I am just too tired, too battle weary,
What did I do wrong? I was just me.

A SOLDIER.

By Andrew Bannerman

A soldier sits on mounds of dust,
And looks upon his hands, at first,
He wonders why he stands alone,
With brothers past, he dreams of home,
A land so free that all can be,
The man that he has chose to be.
Standing tall and firm is he,
To do his duty, so we be free.
And he stands with his brothers true,
His duty he knows he must do.
To deal with all, he swallows hard,
And rises to his feet again,
In his heart his duty true,
To serve, protect and care for you.
So never mock this man you see,
Less we forget his duty true.

FROM THE HEART

The story of a new Invader of our Land
As destructive as War, Though not so grand.

```
P  T  S  D
o  r  t  i
s  a  r  s
t  u  e  o
   m  s  r
   a  s  d
   t     e
   I     r
   C
```

The Awareness of PTSD as told in the words of those suffering from it and their families.

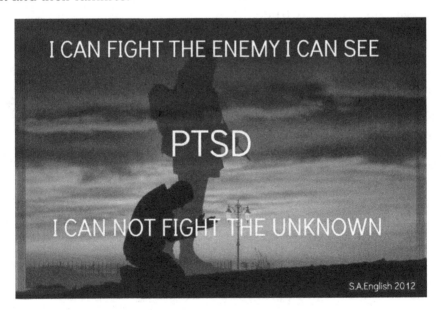

I WHO AM LOST.

I left my guide and lost my way,
Seen sights of which I cannot say.
Had I belief, I would kneel and pray,
But life shows me War holds sway.

We live in conflict large and small,
Each within our self built walls.
To live in peace most have dreamed,
But our Leaders greed, destroy lights beam.
They strive for fame and history's call,
Ignore the cost of innocent who fall.
We fight for Honour, or Faith, but none,
Can be earned through the use of the Gun.
We're told our cause is right and true,
By self-styled mentors, the elite few.
Use us to serve their personal goals,
Both sides claim to save our souls.
The truth is in a mothers arms,
With Mother Earth and all life's charms.
In laughter of young and songs of bird,
The Miracle of life, can always be heard.

I left my guide and lost my way,
Seen sights of which I cannot say.
Had I the Faith I would kneel and pray,
Don't follow me into War's sway.

By
Phil. M. Lamb© 20/3/2012

CROSSMAGLEN.

Province of Ulster.

The day had been bright, full of the sun,
As we followed the border of EIRE.
I'd heard the sweet song of young finches courting,
The fresh smell of cut grass in the air.
We'd been on patrol two weeks today,
Tomorrow stand tour for the town.
It's quiet out here in the fields and the pastures,
But not safe, Hidden eyes all around.

We couldn't enjoy all this sweet green grassland,
We couldn't relax in this place.
For if senses grew dull in the fields and the hedgerows,
Hidden bombs would explode in your face.
The anger and hatred surround and engulf us,
For the length and breadth of this land,
And the people live ever under the mercy,
Of minority terrorist bands.

Peace may return, to this Emerald Island,
In a future as yet unforeseen,
Till then we patrol, nerves steeled to awareness,
Ease the pain of this proud green land.
The danger is present, always and ever,
In this land of the stern Irishmen.
For this town's full of hatred, right up to the border,
In the Province of CROSSMAGLEN.

by Phil. M. Lamb©

EARTH, THIRD OF SOL.

Come speak to me, for I know thee,
Come speak to me, for I hear thee.
Come speak to me and you shall see,
The Mystery of life's great sea.

I'll teach the secrets of the stars,
Of Men of war, the child of Mars.
Of Neptune's ocean, the seas harsh tale,
Of cruel sea monster and gentle whale.
Of birds and flowers, bees and trees,
The knowledge of Gods, from whom Man flees.
Terrestrial Orb, so green and round,
Where Mother Earth's offspring, live, abound.

Come speak to me, for I know thee,
Come speak to me, for I hear thee,
Come speak to me for we have seen,
The Mystery of Life's long dream.

MY LADY FATE.

She glides through lives of living,
Silent she roams the world.
She touches the souls of many,
Her plans for them unfold.
The young men cry, "Who be she?"
The elders warn, "Take care",
For fate be a dark lady,
Aye, Fate be ever there.

Written at school aged 12.

By
Phil. M. Lamb©

FOR SHEILA, OUR WELSH ANGEL, WITH THANKS.

As I sit alone and think of the past,
As I hide within my mind.
As I stay behind my closed windows and doors
Try to leave the world behind.
One day I saw some lines of verse,
Words from a soul so kind.
She told my story and many more,
Helped us see, when all were blind.
 Encouraging us to write our thoughts,
She kept me from going insane.
No words can ever thank this Angel,
She understood the pain.
Now these few lines are not enough,
To thank her as I write,
But thanks to her and others verse,
My darkness fades with light.

Thank you, Itch. Xx

I COULD NOT TAKE A MINUTE MORE

By Taff Evans

I could not take a minute more; I knew I had to die,
My family never wanted me, However hard I tried,
But life goes on beyond the grave; I hear and see you all,
I see you plot and do your worst and wait to see you fall.

My sister turned her back on me. My mother threw me out,
But very soon your day will come: of this I have no doubt,
My sister, I was stood near you, while you gathered at my wake,
Pretending to be full of tears, tears I knew were fake.

Filled with guilt for what you did, you'll never feel at ease,
I'll haunt you till the day you die; you'll feel my icy breeze.
You'll always know when I'm around; you'll be so filled with dread,
The things that I have planned for you, you'll wish that you were dead.

I see you standing at my grave, the visits that you make,
A trip to ease your conscience, tears and words so fake.
I stand beside you, you don't know, kind words you do not say,
I only know you feel the guilt; that helps me on my way.

Dad you never knew the half, of what was going on,
The things your closest, kept from you, as if you don't belong.
But soon the truth will be out, the treachery and lies,
Those so close, the ones you love, won't look you in the eyes.

Now I'm in a better place, there is no hurt or pain,
I'm happy now, so full of love, feel wanted once again.
But even though I'm in this place, a place where others care,
Those who helped to put me here, I'm watching, be aware.

———

CROCODILE TEARS

By Taff Evans

When you're hated by your family and you have no real fiend,
You try to gain their sympathy, through lies which never end.
No matter what the consequence, you do not give a toss,
Your evil tongue will finish you, for us there'll be no loss.

You seem so desperate to be loved, you ruin others lives,
But step back and think a while, at where you throw your knives.
People in glass houses, should never throw a stone,
Your evil lies you spread with ease, will leave you all alone.

You look at other people's lives, and wish it could be you,
But sadly this will never be, your lies you can't undo.
Those people that you chose to hurt, will suffer, and for what,
The reason is they'll lose those things, things you haven't got.

You have the chance to put things right, but truth you do not know,
Prepared to hurt and damage those, each day your lies will grow.
There's those so frail, so close to you, for once just use your head,
Again you'll use your crocodile tears, as they are lying dead.

"IS SUICIDE THE ANSWER"

by Taff Evans

Every man has the right, the right to take his life,
But please remember those left behind, your children and your wife.
Confused and angry, shedding tears, for you they'll weep my friend,
The tragic loss, they can't explain, for them will never end.

The memories that they'll have inside, is all they'll have of you,
The good times and the not so good, things you used to do.
For you my friend, this act you take, so final it will be,
The one who finds you won't forget, the sight that they will see.

Is suicide the answer, there's only you that knows,
But have you thought of talking, before your problem grows.
My friend you know that I am here, all times, both night and day,
Let's sit down and try and make your problems go away.

My friend you've always been there, advice you always gave,
Please don't make me carry you, from hearse toward your grave.
But if you make the choice to go, then carry you I will,
I'll do my best to honour you, until your grave they fill.

No one really knows for sure, the pain and hurt we feel,
But as your friend, I look and see, for you it's very real.
I find it hard to watch you, as you wish your life away,
Please just try and talk things through, let's try and talk today.

TAFF EVANS.

"I have written this poem to highlight some of the problems that our Armed Forces may face once they have been made redundant by our so called government.

The government took them in, trained them to kill another person, kept them on a constant state of high alert and repeatedly put them into conflict and war zones, both home and abroad. Used them for Fire fighting Ambulance crews and Dustbin men during strikes, used them to help those who had been affected by flooding, the list goes on.

"WHERE DID IT ALL GO WRONG"

Just seventeen, I made a choice, a soldier I would be,
I'll join a band of warriors', the world I would now see.
I trained so hard and gave my all; at last I'd made the grade,
For nor I stand ten feet tall, a soldier's now been made.

The years have flew, they've gone so fast, fifteen years now done,
I served in many conflicts, since army life begun.
My time was either training for, or spending time on 'ops,
For in these countries full of hate, I pulled out all the stops.

Many changes to my mind, were made throughout the years,
I felt like a tight-coiled spring, withholding all my fears.
We never had the chance to chill, my senses very high.
Combining training and the 'ops, and thoughts that I would die.

A constant state of high alert, has took its toll on me,
Filled with anger, filled with pain and high anxiety.
I'm so full of all these things, and things I can't explain,
Adrenaline pumping day and night, brings trouble time again.

Discipline, now hard for me, I found it hard to cope,
It got so bad; I served in jail, from now on there's no hope.
The Army took me as a boy, and made me what I am today,
But when my time in jail was done, I was discharged straight away.

I felt so hurt, I felt so sad, where had it all gone wrong?
Not a thing was put in place to help me get along.
I had no place to go and live, which left me on the street,
A place so cold and dangerous, no trust those I'd meet.

Trouble seemed to follow me, while living rough outdoors,
Time and time I fought with others in shop doors,
The police they came so many times, I tell the same old tale,
But now they've had enough of me, I'm in a civvy jail.

Sentence done, they've let me go, I'm back to living rough,
Trying hard to find a place, but life out here's so tough.
People stare at what I am; they don't know what I had been,
There's none who know I served my country and my Queen.

I wonder now, what was it for, the thoughts they hurt my head,
For I have been to hell and back, and dealt with mates now dead.
Never in you wildest dreams, could you go where I've been,
Picking up bits of friends, such sights you've never seen.

I haven't had a wash or shave, nor have I changed my clothes,
I smell and feel afraid of life, but no one ever knows.
Possessions that I have are few, but mean the world to me,
Things of sentimental value, memories just for me.

Not so very long ago, in uniform starched and pressed,
I stood within the ranks of men, so clean and smartly dressed.
But now within my dirty coat; the treasures I hold dear,
For in my pocket are my medals, held from yesteryear.

Christmas time is here again, a time of festive cheer,
For me I have no friends or family, no one close or dear.
But when you see me in my doorway, lying on the floor,
Please do not look down on me, or hurt me anymore.

This life I lead I did not choose, I wish I were like you,
Oh what I'd give to have a house, with family things to do.
A place of safety, place of warmth, a place that's filled with love,
I ask for this each night I pray, to the good Lord up above.

I never had to beg before; it goes against the grain,
When people laugh and jeer at me, time and time again.
Oh how I wish, there was a place, or someone that would care,
Please God, send me someone, please answer this my prayer.

"MAY GOD BLESS OUR ARMED FORCES AND THOSE MEN AND
WOMEN OF THE CHARITY 'SOLDIERS OFF THE STREET'"

MY DEAR SON ASHLEY
By Mary Fells

I feel so alone,
Because the pain I'm feeling,
Is never going to leave me alone.
You came to see me, on that terrible day,
But the look in your eyes,
You were so far away.
As I lay awake at night,
I really try to understand your plight,
All the things that you saw,
Because you did your duty and went to war.
So Government, it's time to hang your heads in shame,
Because my sons death, will not be in vane.
Time to come and do what's right,
Because our Soldiers never gave up the fight,
Don't be ignorant to what our boys do,
To give our country freedom,
For the likes of You.
You must give our forces,
The help they deserve,
Because they were Proud to serve.

Rest in peace, my beautiful son,
I will love you, always,
From your loving Mum.

THE MEN IN CAMO GREEN.

By Andy Bannerman, 26/08/2012

A man stood still in camo green,
His gear is checked, it gets called in,
The job, to see what has become,
Of places seen, but not revealed,
And off he sets, with brothers true,
To keep the peace they earn for you.
And as they march by, in slow time,
Their heads confused, by what they've seen,
Never do they get to see,
The end result of life they gave.
As in a flash, it starts again,
And rounds fly by and hit the ground,
They squat and take a peek around,
To see if all their mates are found,
And if by chance, they all are well,
They rise once more and start to walk,
In single file, along the road,
That only few have seen or read,
Until they come upon their home,
And lay their weary heads down fast,
To sleep and think of things they love.
Of family love, and home once more,
Until the call comes once again,
To raise themselves and go Again.

Hi I'm Sheila English, as a sufferer of PTSD, I found that writing my poetry helped me cope. I wanted to find a way to help others who suffered this so I set up the group to see if it could. It started as a simple page on Facebook, From the Heart Poetry page and it's success has astonished us all. It has gone from strength to strength, with many who had never thought of writing poems, finding it, well I guess therapeutic. We now believe there are poets hiding in all of us especially deep within, as our work shows. We support each other, both ex-service personnel, their families and others. There are many causes of PTSD but little awareness. Now there is a great increase in sufferers from the Armed services returning from conflicts abroad, as in the days of the two world wars, Korea, Vietnam, the Falklands, Northern Ireland, Kuwait, Iraq and ongoing in Afghanistan. There are many from civilian life as a result of Assaults, accidents and tragic loss. PTSD is an Invisible disability but none the less damaging, for the sufferer And their families. They Need understanding, they Deserve respect and they need our awareness. Most of all thanks must go to Phil for getting our poems published. Through this we will be able to help our chosen charities for Ex- service men and women and all who suffer from this invisible illness. Thank you, please I hope you enjoy our humble writings.

S.A. English.

ptsd
I am here

can you see me
I am a statistic the government
say's does not exist

dedicated to a dear friend , hope you find your way home

s.a.english 2012

CHILDREN OUTCAST.

The children no-one wanted,
Do you know who we are.
Or are we just those little brats,
In the big house by the park.
They not normal, that's why they there,
Minibus to school, the parents stand and stare.
Can't read or write, can only steal,
They must be evil, they don't feel.
Ignore them the mothers say,
Why don't the council send them away.
Don't lower your gaze these thugs can't hurt,
Keep rubbing their faces in the dirt.
But if you took time to ask them why,
You'd find little Josie scared and shy.
Young Peter standing, angry and curt,
Lets no-one close then you don't get hurt.
Teen Maisy, sad, sour and surly,
Because She was daddys 'Special Girly',
These kids in care carry the shame,
Of their parents anger and cruel blame.
They've done nothing wrong so please be fair,
Things done to THEM is why they're in care.

By Phil. M. Lamb© *12/07/2012*

The 30th. Anniversary of the Falklands may their sacrifice not be forgotten.

Lost comrades, Lost Friends.

Where are Ray, Chalky and John,
They were here in San Carlos,
Lord, where have they gone

We drank together on that journey down,
We trained on the decks, or just messed around.
We sat playing cards, or boasting of birds,
Gossiped on what the staff clerks had heard.
We knew what was coming least we thought we did,
Christ, we knew nothing, just wide-eyed green kids.
Those faceless men in their plush velvet seats,
Sent us far from home where death we must meet.

Ray lost his belly, cut wide by grenade,
He died on a rock, his blood a cascade.
We gave him some smokes, said soon you'll be home,
As he died masked our feelings, then left him alone.
We'd trained for this, these past ten years,
Touched it in Ireland, but shed few tears.
We thought we knew all to be known,
Soldiers trained true, men full grown.

Where are Ray, Chalky and John,
They were here in San Carlos,
Lord, where have they gone.

At Fitzroy burned John on Galahads deck,

Flame burned him black, from feet to his neck.
They drink their brandy in rich dining hall,
Read war reports, worried shares might fall.
But We can't except the price that we paid,
As we count the cost at the end of the day.
Men of both sides, both young and old,
How easily, cheaply, their lives had been sold.

On Harriet mount, Chalky drained blood,
Green ghosts in their trenches, cut him down in the mud.
I couldn't be with him, to ease his pain,
I was hit on Mount William, but who is to blame.
Not the soldiers we fought, not those scared young men,
But political leaders who start wars with a pen.
They profit from conflict, in wealth and power,
While they sit in splendour in their ivory tower.
Hide previous knowledge, with political intrigue,
Cover indecision and cloak their own greed.

There are Ray, Chalky and John,
They were killed in the Falklands,
Lord, why have they gone.

By Phil. M. Lamb© *28/3/2012*

Written during recession of 1983-84

DOLE QUEUE BLUES.

The night it is lonely, cold and dark,
The breeze of solitude be stark.
The night is long for morn to come,
No hurry, no work, no need to run.
Another day will born for naught,
Another day for work is sought,
Another day of fruitless seek,
Another day, another week.

A new invader stalks our land,
As deadly as war,though not so grand.
Three million lost,the papers say,
The numbers rise, grow everyday.
Unemployment rules this land of mine,
Young see no future, and turn to crime.
Toxteth,Brixton and Tottenham are,
Riot town theatres of racial war.

Child killings, rapes and murders grow,
Police corruption the criminals crow.
The men of the media, show us the face,
The malicious breakdown of our civilized race.
With internal decay of Europe, the world,
Comes the great final conflict, that many foretold.
Do we have a future, in our cultural collapse,
And will mankind survive this Dinosaur lapse.

The planet is changing, technology has won,
Automation takes meaning,from man and his son.
There are Robots for labor, and Computers to rule,
But what will our children and their children do.

Now leisure is limited, and boredom immense,
Depression increasing, unrest grows intense.
Suicides climb, insanity's high,
The conflict of man and machine soon will rise.

The race of man rebels and wars,
Against the governing of machines and their laws.
They fight for free thought, and the meaning of life,
To ensure that our human mind can survive.
For the brain of man must be active and bright,
To evolve to the perfection of celestial light.
Then reach that elusive astral plane,
And earn them their place in Universal reign.

But night now is waning, and dawn soon will break,
Birds begin singing, the people awake.
Have I seen our future in dreams of the mind,
Is this the start of the end of mankind.
Yet morn has arrived and a new day begun,
My thoughts they are breaking, at sight of the Sun.
The sky it is changing, dark grays to light blue,
These thoughts I have written,
Just the DOLE QUEUE BLUES.
By Phil. M. Lamb©

THE EYES
By Sheila English 24/06/2012

Look into my eyes,
What do you see.
When I say I'm fine,
Can that really be,
Look again.
Now look into my soul,
Do you see it now,
I am no longer whole,
When I smile.
Does it reach the eyes,
Or echo my mournful cries,
Next time you look,
Take a little longer,
I may need your help,
Till I am stronger.

A smiling face sometimes lies,
The truth is there,
It's in the eyes.

PTSD . . . REFLECTION IN A MIRROR.

By Sheila English 20/06/2012

Dressed in number ones looking ever so smart,
Looks in the mirror,
Tears in his eyes an ache in his heart.
He is back in the past,
Fear etched on his face,
His heart beating at a tremendous pace,
Cradling his mate covered in blood,
Freezing cold, laying in the mud,
This was war, it was never a game,
For this ex-soldier, life can never be the same.
They both survived,
And the flesh wounds they healed,
But the mind never did,
At the bottom of a bottle he hid,
Till he looked in a mirror and saw what he saw,
He let out a criminal roar,
Convulsing in tears, he fell to the floor.

NO MAN IS AN ISLAND . . . WE ALL NEED SOMEONE.

Sheila English 18/06/2012

Today I was an island,
Nobody was around,
I stood there all alone,
I was on shaky ground,
Looking all around me,
Emptiness everywhere,
Who was there to care for me,
Who would hear my prayer,
Then I remembered,
I looked to heaven above,
Smiling down at me was,
A face so full of love.
Thank you Lord.

PTSD . . . LETTER TO THE GOVERNMENT

Sheila English 07/07/2012

I am on a bender,
I've smashed up my phone,
Don't want to talk to you,
Just leave me alone,
I don't want your sympathy,
Why don't you go away.
Leave me to my misery
I don't want to play,
You say come on soldier,
Why don't you grow some balls,
Well you don't really know me,
In fact you know f*** all.
You weren't there for me,
When my best friend died,
You weren't there for me,
As night after night I cried,
You weren't there when I wanted a friend,
And you weren't there when my eyes closed,
Sorry mate ....To late ...The end.

IN THE FLICKERING CANDLELIGHT

Sheila English 23/06/2012

In the flickering candlelight,
In the flickering flame,
Into the darkness of the night,
I silently call your name.
Is it you that I see?
As I call through time and space,
Or is it just my grief for you,
That makes me see your face,
In the flickering candlelight,
In the flickering flame,
Into the darkness of the night,
I tearfully call your name.

PTSD

Sheila English 27/05/2012

My daddy don't mean to make me cry,
He went away and saw friends die,
Mummy says he is not well,
And talks about a living hell,
When Daddy is unhappy,
He shouts at me and starts to yell,
Is this the place mummy calls hell.
Can I have my old daddy please,
Not the one with,
What does mummy call it?
PTSD.

MY FRIEND YOU TOOK YOUR LIFE TODAY.

By Taff Evans

My friend you took your life today, why, we'll never know,
Had your problems got so great; you thought you had to go.
We never saw you troubled; you always had a smile,
Always there to help us all, to go that extra mile.

The signs they say, are always there, but we don't always see,
There's never once we saw these signs, or what was soon to be.
My friend, if we could turn back time, your problems you might tell,
Professional help and all our love, just might have made you well.

The sadness that you leave behind, you never could have known,
Memories of the good old days, the special seeds you've sown.
You touched our hearts in many ways, but sadly now you've gone,
But we will always think of you, with us you still belong.

Special nights and special days, our thoughts will be with you,
We'll think of all the things we did, that no one ever knew.
My friend, the world that your now in, you will not suffer pain,
You've paved the way, and wait for us, till we meet again.

MY FRIEND
By Taff Evans

The sound like thunder all around, the ground it trembled to the sound,
Shots were also heard that day, those shots that took your life away.
The Angels came and took you home, but left your wife and kids alone.
Oh my friend, what price you paid, the selfless acts that you had made.

For Ulster's sake your life you gave, and now we take you to your grave,
With honour, pride and hidden dread, it hit us all that you are dead.
The hearse arrives; the family sobbed, for you my friend, whose life was robbed,
Our final act we give our best, we carry you and lay to rest.

Your wife and children, now alone, ask why God has called you home,
The cruel way your life was lost, does not make sense, a tragic loss.
My friend with fondness, teary eyes, I know you look down from the skies,
Today is yours, a special day, a well-earned rest, for you we pray.

For those of us, that's left behind, forever in our thought and mind,
There will always be so true, a vacant space, which once was you.
With danger lurking all around, the call to arms, your future found,
My friend you never let us down, when we all wore the Harp and Crown.

MY CHINESE LANTERN
By Taff Evans

The night is still and very cold, no clouds up in the sky,
I sit alone, remember things, from days that's now gone by,
For each and every star that twinkles, in this clear night sky,
Are souls of Heroes, family, friends, who sadly had to die.

As my memories reappear, a tear forms in my eye,
God, you took them all away, I'm sad and wonder why.
Yet even though they had to go, I feel them very near,
The thoughts and memories of them all, I hold so very dear.

Oh what I'd give to have you all, back here with me tonight,
But in a sense you are with me, you're shining very bright.
There's many things I should have said, before you went away,
But every day and every night, I tell you when I pray.

Tonight is a special night, I see you all above,
I'll send a special prayer to you, a prayer that's filled with love.
I have a Chinese lantern, there's many things I'll write,
You'll all know what my thoughts will be, on this special night.

There's many words, I had to write, before I let it go,
Those things, those very special things, you never got to know.
The words are now complete my friends, and silently I cry,
I watch my Chinese Lantern burn, to meet you in the sky.

PADRE.

By Taff Evans.

Padre I have served for years, and always bottled up my fears,
But now I tremble, often weep, and times afraid to got to sleep.
For in my heart and in my soul, it's hard to play the soldiers role,
To no one else, I cannot speak, in case they think I'm feeling weak.

Padre now I'm far from home, I've never felt so all alone,
In Afghans hot and burning sand, a war I cannot understand.
The sound of battle always near, with every bomb I shake with fear,
Then bullets fly, I hear their crack, without a thought, I fire back.

Padre now I'm back on tour, I feel I cannot take much more,
I thought a veteran such as me, could cope with what I do and see.
But even though I show no fear, I feel like death is always near,
My family, sadly far away, are in my thoughts through night and day.

Padre there's two sides of me, the side I hide, the side mates see,
Fore mates I'll always give my best, I'll be right up there with the rest.
But in this hot and burning sand, I need a guide and helping hand,
Padre say a prayer with me, a prayer for mates and family.

"In Nomine Patris, Et Filii, Et Spiritus Sancti. Amen"

MASTER.

By Taff Evans

Master I have set upon, a journey through my life,
I ask that you will walk with me, in good times and in strife.
My journey starts with just one step, with many more to come,
But Master there are years ahead, to get my learning done.

Master teach me wisdom, to know what's right and wrong,
That I may see the difference, and meet them both head on.
Wisdom means the choice I'd made by thinking things right through,
But wisdom also means that I, may know what's false and true.

Master teach me courage, to face what lies ahead,
The trying times, the fear and pain and times of total dread.
Dangerous times, they wait for me, yet I must fight the fear,
To do what's right, against all odds, when trying times appear.

Master teach me honesty, that I will be sincere,
To those I meet along the way, and those that I hold dear.
I search my heart for answers; yet question what I hear,
Master when such things arise, it's then I'd like you near.

Master now my journey starts, there's such a lot to learn,
But now I take each step with you, for knowledge that I yearn.
My answers lie from deep within, from deep within my soul,
Master, walk along with me, to help me reach my goal.

YEARS AND TEARS.

By Sue Ross.

Years may have passed, but the tears still fall,
I remember the times, when we had it all.
Love, time, laughter, joy and a future both,
But war stripped you of hopes and dreams,
Our love faltered, I couldn't hear your silent screams.
I carry the guilt of not being there, your last day,
All I can say, I was young, not like today.
Rest easy my love, for I now understand,
You no longer suffer; hold my heart in your hand.

Found by Roy Humphries, author unknown.

TERRIBLE DREAMS.

I woke up this morning from a terrible dream,
Sweating profusely, I wanted to scream.
More bad memories flooding into my mind,
The type that you wanted to just leave behind,

Thinking of the horrors of some years ago,
Horrors that seem to pass ever so slow,
Remembering my brothers, having to got through such pain.
And knowing that I would never see them again.

I have been very lucky, these past thirty years,
Being able to bury the memories and fears,
Thinking back to those days, listening to brothers speak,
Remembering so much, from that epic week.

A cold May Day in nineteen eighty two,
The sky so overcast, a cold morning dew,
Looking around, how many brothers were there,
Seeing so many missing, wishing I didn't care.

Wondering how this could have happened to me,
Realizing the price we pay to be free,
But to lose so many men, so many boys,
Thrown away like so many broken toys.

Politicians sitting in their offices, so smug,
Tossing war reports on their desks, with a shrug,
Complaining of snow and the difficult drive,
Wondering if they'll miss the Chambers party at five.

Caring only that they've won another term,
By God this year, they'll get a raise, on that they're firm,
In a home in Britain, there's a knock on a door,
The Padre to say, your son won't be home anymore.

To the window you his picture for all to see,
Your husband, your son, died so they could be free,
Buried in a hole in the frozen far flung land,
You sit down and cry, your head in your hands.

Soldiers come home broken, some with trench-ridden feet,
Hands shaking so hard, can't hold utensils to eat,
Trying to put lives back together, to forget it all,
Sitting in chair, glassy eyes, staring at the wall.

Being so moody, so withdrawn, never speaking at all,
Shutting down all the memories, wait for the doctor to call,
Yes I woke with these memories in 2012,
These memories of the Falklands, I will forever hold.